SUMMARY:

Tell Me More

Stories About the 12 Hardest Things I'm

Learning to Say

ABBEY BEATHAN

Legal & Disclaimer

The information contained in this book is not designed to replace or take the place of any form of medicine or professional medical advice. The information in this book has been provided for educational and entertainment purposes only.

The information contained in this book has been compiled from sources deemed reliable, and it is accurate to the best of the Author's knowledge; however, the Author cannot guarantee its accuracy and validity and cannot be held liable for any errors or omissions. Changes are periodically made to this book. You must consult your doctor or get professional medical advice before using any of the suggested remedies, techniques, or information in this book. Images used in this book are not the same as of that of the actual book. This is a totally separate and different entity from that of the original book titled: "Tell Me More".

Upon using the information contained in this book, you agree to hold harmless the Author from and against any damages, costs, and expenses, including any legal fees potentially resulting from the application of any of the information provided by this guide. This disclaimer applies to any damages or injury caused by the use and application, whether directly or indirectly, of any advice or information presented, whether for breach of contract, tort, negligence, personal injury, criminal intent, or under any other cause of action.

You agree to accept all risks of using the information presented inside this book. You need to consult a professional medical practitioner in order to ensure you are both able and healthy enough to participate in this program.

Table of Contents

The Book at a Glance v

It's Like This 1

Tell Me More 3

I Don't Know 5

I Know 7

No 9

Yes 13

I Was Wrong 14

Good Enough 17

I Love You 21

No Words At All 22

Onward 25

This Is It 30

Conclusion 32

Final Thoughts 39

About the Author 47

Final Thoughts 48

The Book at a Glance

It's Like This – This chapter will introduce you to Kelly, a fifty-year-old woman with her hardworking husband Edward, two teenage daughters, Georgia and Claire, moving on Mom, meditation guy Will, and her most loved Dad Greenie.

Tell Me More – Kelly started her day with a facial and a *tell me more* talk with Tish. Do you know the power of listening? Have you tried asking questions rather than telling or sharing your own ideas? In this chapter, Kelly will realize the true meaning and value of listening.

I Don't Know – In the midst of grieving, Kelly found out that like her dad, Greenie, she also became a victim of cancer. Sometimes, it's better to admit the things that you don't know. After all, have you tried to ask yourself, "Do I really need to know?"

I Know – Her father was dead. Her best friend passed away. Both important persons, both died for the same reason. Kelly had an understanding of grieving. She made ways on how to still remember her beloved Greenie and Liz. With the encounter of people in the summer camp she attended, she realized the relevance of knowing and loving.

No – In this chapter, Kelly will share with us some of her experiences that taught her how to turn down cowardice when saying *no*. These experiences include her tenth birthday, conversation with her mom and friend, and the hopeful day of convincing her better half for extending their family of having more children.

Yes – What things does Kelly say *yes* to? Here's the revelation...

I Was Wrong – Did you come to a point when the circumstances suggest that you should confess and admit your wrongdoing? What did you feel? Did you feel guilty, angry, or relieved? Kelly, from her dog discipline issues, to her daughter not flushing the toilet properly, until the death of someone close to her heart realized the real meaning and message of the words *I was wrong*.

Good Enough – Kelly, on her teenage days, faced a lot of rejections and frustrations. Because of these sudden events, when faced with a diverged road, will she take the path of acceptance or enter the way to rebellion? Find out what happened to her when she learned from the people around her and her experiences that, in life, it is alright to say: *Okay. I'm good enough*.

I Love You – How often do you say these words? To whom

do you tell these - to your parents? Siblings? Children? Friends? Or boyfriend slash girlfriend? Kelly told these words many times to many people. From the usual reasons, she expressed her own. She also proved that when you love, you also forgive. Come. Read and be loved.

No Words At All – Kelly, known as someone who has a lot of interesting stories to tell, learned to make either a pause or a stop from talking. From her own perspective and from the things that she has learned, an important point comes out that there is still a way to communicate to others even without speaking or telling. What will this way be? Did it help Kelly? Was it used by her as another form of communication? Expect some of Kelly's and her fiend's words with this chapter entitled *No Words At All*.

Onward – Kelly wrote a heart melting and warming letter to her beloved best friend, Liz. She mentioned there a lot of incredible and worth sharing stories. These stories comprised of the annual tradition, Andy (Liz's better half), Liz's kids, Kelly's extended family, Andy's and Edward's conversation about mothers, the bedside, Andy's possibility of having a crush, the day Liz passed away, the memorial, and lastly, the Apollo 13's Mission. Why did she write a letter knowing that it was impossible for her dead best friend to read it? Was it her way of telling that she missed her best friend very much?

Be ready to be moved with Kelly's touching, friendly, and lovely letter.

This Is It – Kelly reminisced the times when she dreamed of everything she wanted during her college days. Fast forward to her thirties and forties when she stepped up to the level of parenthood and motherhood. Will she wish to come back to the older days where enjoyment was on the top of the list or prefer to knock and enter the door of serious life, where challenges await?

It's Like This

It was actually a fine morning to start the day for others but it wasn't for Kelly. She was haunted by that forlorn fact that the person she loved the most, Greenie, her dad, passed away. She kept thinking that death really was inevitable but also hoping the possibility of having her dad back.

Kelly has two teenage daughters, Georgia and Claire. Georgia, sixteen years of age, likes lacrosse, Snapchat, pre-calculus, chemistry, and dancing. She likes to tell captivating stories to her mom. Claire, on the other hand, a fourteen-year-old girl, plays volleyball, basketball, decorates baked goods, and throws parties – a creative genius, as her mom calls her.

Edward, Kelly's better half, is a man who loves swimming, fanboys the Golden State Warriors, likes the grocery store and stove (meaning household chores), and even helps her color the back of her hair.

Kelly is a fifty-year old woman who is very conscious about the way she looks and preoccupied with the ideas she has. She has built furniture, has been a photographer, and has started a company which did not give her any satisfaction at all, except for the children's local hospital where she volunteered to take care of babies.

Mary Corrigan, Kelly's mother, did spend her precious time in anything that she wanted and needed. She wanted to play games, so she did and enjoyed doing it. She needed privacy, church, and time for herself, including her beloved husband's bank account. Did she grieve over her husband's loss? Yes. But looking at her doing the things that she wanted and needed, it made Kelly think of how could her mother do those things yet she, on the other hand, was still haunted by her father's absence.

Whenever Kelly remembered something that was at the verge of forgetting, she would get mad easily. "Why am I so mad at everyone?" she would say.

Until one day, she had a conversation with a man named Will, also known as the meditation guy and an officemate of her husband's. With his inspirational quotes about life, he brought enlightenment to Kelly of what life really was.

Tell Me More

Kelly had her facial one day with Tish, the facial expert. Kelly, who's known as someone who has a lot issues to rant about in life, started this simple talk with Tish, which became a friendly conversation along the way. Whenever Kelly finished a topic, Tish would ask for more without any butt in part. This made Kelly feel grateful. This made her feel that someone was there to listen to her.

She also had an encounter with a friend named Tracy. Both of them were having the concern of whether to let their young adults decide for themselves to be independent or not. At the midst of their conversation, Georgia called telling about her classmates' issues. This became Kelly's mission. Like what Tish did and with the help of Tracy's suggestions, little by little, she learned to listen to her daughter to make her feel important without giving any advice at all.

When it was the couple who talked about *telling more*, they both agreed that it really did make them wonder what else people might tell if they would just keep asking questions without telling their insights.

This *telling me more* made Kelly also remember her

unforgettable conversation with her dad. He shared with her his encounter with their family priest, who was dying. Father Reinfert told how he felt grateful for someone to visit and listen to him. "Your visit meant a lot", said the nun to Greenie after the priest's death.

I Don't Know

Kelly's friend, Mary Hope, was full of hope about having a child of her own. She got pregnant the first, second, and third time, yet no single little angel to be carried in her loving arms. MH and her husband came to a point where a sea of questions raised about the heart-wrenching events. Nevertheless, they realized that instead of asking the *Whys*, they chose the *Why nots*. They've tried the alternatives from medical solution to the process of adoption.

Carrying the baby named Eliza as if her own from the beginning, MH would tell Kelly, "I don't know who this kid is, but so far, I can tell you that she knows how to get what she wants". After a dozen of years, she would say, "I don't know who this kid is, but she does. She knows exactly who she is. I'm just along for the ride." What MH said marked question marks to Kelly.

Same with MH, a sudden change happened. It was when the sickness called Cancer came to Kelly's life. She and her husband, Edward, termed it as The Enemy, the treatment as A Journey, and Kelly herself as A Hero.

Being a cancer patient, she believed that people might just say three things to her: either *You're so brave*, *Was it in your family?* or *What a wake-up call*. Instead of grieving, Kelly chose to think about the things that she had done to remind herself why she got it.

She had an encounter with a friend of hers, Sarah, a pediatrician. From Sarah's perspective, she would tell Kelly that it's okay to say *I don't know*, that something can just be explained by those three words – that something happened because it can.

Another thought that crossed her mind was during the special day of hers and her better half's lives – their wedding. Uncle Jimmy's speech gave her a thought that you have to learn to accept that life is a mystery. This also leads to acceptance of the fact that there were things that she didn't and couldn't know.

I Know

To befriend Liz, Edward's friend's wife, was not that easy before for Kelly. Time came, and despite their differences, they became close friends. They did build a friendship more like sisters.

Until one day, Liz found out that she had cancer. Yes, she was dying. She was someone who would spend a limited time here on Earth. When she told about this Cancer the Enemy to Kelly, she would tell her that she couldn't take it anymore, that she was too tired and in pain. She also wished to die in her bed.

The only words that came out Kelly's mouth were *I know*. She knew how Liz's husband, Andy, and kids felt about her dying situation. She knew it because it reminded her of her most loved dad, Greenie, who had faced also The Enemy and The Death.

A few days after Liz's and Kelly's conversation, it did happen. Liz passed away. She died in her bed.

A summer camp was organized for people, particularly kids whose parents died of cancer, victims of The Enemy. Kelly volunteered to lead journaling projects and writing workshops for kids. This was her way of staying close to her dad and to Liz. Everyone in the camp knew how it felt to lose someone they loved so much. Like everybody, she loved her dad and her friend so very much.

"There's no one right way to feel bad, to want something you can't have. And there's no one right way to feel better", said Lucy, a twelve-year-old girl who seemed young for the gift of her tongue. Kelly had the chance to talk to Lucy. Both of them were grieving for their losses. Both of them agreed that it was better to hear the words *I know* than *I'm sorry*. Both of them knew how it felt that sad feeling of looking for someone who was not around anymore.

On the other hand, Kelly felt lucky to know her friend Liz more to know more about other people. She believed that once you known a person, you will have the chance to be loved. To be loved just by saying *I know*.

No

On The day of her ninth birthday, Kelly had a lot of plans for her tenth birthday celebration. She shared her thoughts with her mom and dad. A pool party came to her mind, which she happily shared with them. Her mom doubted it but her dad was all for it. It would have been a good idea to have Mrs. Mather's (pool owner) permission for this exciting and well-planned celebration. Unfortunately, a month before her birthday, her friend Allison celebrated her tenth special day through a pool party with a pool of her own, so she decided not to have this kind of party anymore.

Her mom suggested to have the party in their basement instead. It was actually a ridiculous idea for Kelly. Her mom added to also having a *literal* pool party in there with the *pool table* of her brothers. Thinking that she had no choice at all, she was about to agree on that idea yet in her one condition. She would go for it yet she would want her friends to have hoagies for food. She used to see her mom eating hoagies for a few days a week, so it gave her the idea that it was okay to have them, and also for her friends.

Her mom didn't buy it. She said *no* for Kelly's request. Hoagies were replaced by cheese pizza and a chocolate cake.

This was when Kelly told, admitted or white lied to her mom that she was allergic to cheese. She said that it was since forever that she didn't like it at all. This unbelievable excuse made her hate cheese and intentionally be allergic to it for a decade. She kept waiting for her mom to apologize because Kelly thought that it was her mom's fault to ruin her plan B birthday party. Unfortunately, it didn't really happen. There was no chance of *mother apologizing to her daughter* act at all. It was as if her mom's *no* was made with dignity.

Kelly, now a mother of two wonderful daughters, remembered this cheese issue between her and her mom. For her, it would be better to change how she would handle being a mother of two. How would they like her was one of her top concerns. For her, saying *yes* was fun. Saying *yes* made you be loved by the people you love. This was totally different and opposite to how her mom would react when a daughter asked for something costly or pricey.

A recollection came up to Kelly about her twenties. It was when her cousin bravely asked whether her parents were divorced or just not living together anymore. It made Kelly confused about how could someone just tell or notice it just by observing or looking at how people acted. This cousin of hers would just tell her that he used to see her dad but never saw her mom with him. She remembered the times when they would go to church or somewhere having two cars – her dad's and her mom's. Her mom would also do things that confused Kelly, whether she was used to doing things others didn't like or just doing it because that's what she wanted to do. Would it be enough to say that they were separated?

When she had the chance to talk to Mrs. Corrigan, Kelly knew and learned that being in love and intact with marriage didn't mean that you agreed on the same things, that you should do the same hobbies. She told her daughter that her father was more of mingling with other people, while she was satisfied being on her own. She also reminded that she still loved, loves, and will love her husband dearly.

Her mom would freely say what she wanted. That's why her daughter and two sons perceived to ask her about the gift that she would like to get on her birthday, because she used to even write and post what she wished to have. Unlike now, the only thing she wished from her children was for them to tell their problems that she could handle or could lend help, and if she couldn't help in any form, she would just want a worry-free and full of sleep life as a gift.

With this delightful conversation with her mom, Kelly had another talk with a friend of hers, who told and made her realize to learn to say *no* without complaining and explaining.

That it was possible to say this word nicely and still be loved.

Kelly, despite of her Cancer The Enemy, had also planned of having two more children. She did research a lot of possibilities and alternatives like what her friend MH did, since Kelly couldn't get pregnant anymore. With this plan and out of respect, she told Edward about it. She got another *no*, not from her mom but from her husband. He assured her that their family was enough for him and it was okay to declare limits in a relationship.

Yes

Kelly just shared all the things that made her happy. One particular part of the list was when she mentioned that she wanted a kid who would want to sleep with them. It was obvious indeed how she wanted to have someone that she couldn't possibly have.

I Was Wrong

Discipline per se was very hard to create for Kelly, based on her personality. It was hard to contain even for a pet dog that she raised. Her husband would tell her, "You won't monitor and correct the behavior, it's about having consistency for kids." For kids? Since this was mentioned, she remembered what happened when her emotions turned upside down because of what she used to see in the toilet – someone won't flush it, which would invite Hershey, the pet dog, to eat or drink whatever was in that toilet. "How has my life come to this?" Kelly would ask herself while cleaning the mess in the comfort room. One day, out of having an authority attitude, she talked to her daughters about the *flushing routine* and asserted that she would never ever clean that kind of mess again. Georgia admitted that, sometimes, she would try, but couldn't flush that properly or it was hard to do it though it seemed easy.

Until one day, out of a very calm day, she thought, Kelly noticed The Mess again. She stormed and ferociously shouted about it as if cleaning the comfort room and cleaning The Mess were the only things she had been doing all her life – like there was a treasure that she had been taking care of and in a split second someone took it like that was too easy to take. Georgia, who had an advanced thought that her mother would blame her, seriously and undoubtedly said that she didn't do it. Claire, on the other hand, without confirming whether she did it or didn't, suggested that she would clean the mess. Instead of letting Claire do the volunteered act, Kelly became more furious and asked Georgia to do the cleaning instead because she believed that Georgia did not admit what she had done. Edward found it ridiculous for blaming Georgia for something that Kelly didn't even see what happened. Until one day, out of shyness, but with a touch of bravery, Claire talked to her mom and admitted that it was her doing and not Georgia's, that she lost confidence in telling the truth because she was afraid of what emotion her mom had shown on that day.

Knowing the truth because of Claire's confession, Kelly thought that she needed to do an act of apology to Georgia. She reminisced the lesson her mom used to tell her about apology. That is should be near-perfect, must be felt, and must be properly conveyed. That it should be served plain, just like saying *I'm sorry* without any further explanation at all. Thinking about childhood days, particularly kindergarten, kids ask a lot of questions. It's as if these words would just bring the conversation into a lot of endless questions of *whys* and *how's*. What she just told Georgia was the line *I was wrong.*

15

This incident with her daughter gave Kelly the chance to remember Cleta, her father's mother, her grandmother. She didn't spend much time visiting her grandmother. If she did, she would tell her dad Greenie and it would instantly make him happy. Until days came and no visitation was paid to her. Kelly was in shock with the news from her dad that her dear Cleta passed away.

"You should have gone regularly, Kelly. She was your grandmother." This line of Greenie was like a punch or a slap on her face. How powerful this line was that she cried because of shame more than because of her grandmother's death. She felt terrible indeed. Again, when she had the chance to talk to her dad, she said *I was wrong*. She also told him that she was selfish for not paying a visit to Cleta.

What her father responded was that it was important to do it because his mom was old. *Now you know* was the second slapping line that she heard from him.

Good Enough

Ariel, a smart and successful psychotherapist friend of Kelly had a meaningful talk with her one day. She loved to listen to people's stories. Good listening was on the top of her qualities whether as a friend, a doctor, or a person, so that meant thirty hours a week would be okay for her to listen professionally to the people or patients she used to talk to. For her dedication and excellence, undergraduate studies were not enough for her. She still pursued her Ph.D. During these many studying days, a practicum was required for her to pass before the licensing. It meant interviewing a lot of people to complete three thousand hours to treat them. Despite her perseverance in her chosen career, despite the fact that she was smart, she was still in doubt of herself. She was about to turn it down. She had a chance to talk to her instructor, Laura, that she couldn't do it. She was in doubt on how could a twenty-four-year-old be trusted with people's life issues and stories, especially the ones that were very hard to share, entrusted to, or even to remember. However, Laura seriously talked to her and assured her that she was trustworthy and the mere fact that she was being trusted was *good enough*. She did go for it. One particular interview that she had and couldn't forget was with a person named Jean.

Jean had a lot of horrible things that she shared with and entrusted to Ariel. Her family had been killed. She was raped, which resulted in having a son.

Leaving her with that kind of story made Ariel think that that was enough to take. She also felt that she was the only one who was able to listen to Jean. Laura's assurance of Ariel being the trustworthy person was eventually true.

Ariel's daughter, Ruby, participated in the bar mitzvah. This was a Jewish activity wherein she sang in Hebrew and told stories to people about the Old Testament. Kelly and her daughters were present during that event. Kelly was amazed by how Ruby was raised. She even compared what this teenager knew and what her daughters were familiar with.

After the ceremony, Kelly had conversed with Rabbi Michael, the husband of Rabbi Noa, who guided Ruby through this Jewish stuff.

She was curious about why was their community particularly for children who were in their or about to turn thirteen. According to him, this was not just the age where physical appearances changed and intellectual aspect developed, it was more of letting the teenagers discovered their own *power*. This power pertained to the moment when these teenagers decided for themselves on how they would contribute positively in changing the world. On how they would be courageous in voicing out what's inside. On how they could make a difference.

At thirteen, Kelly remembered that her teachers liked her and she even did not lie that much to her parents, but what she remembered most was on her fifteenth. She worked at a pizza parlor, which seemed like a taken-for-granted opportunity for her, because she used to go to work late or waste time chatting a lot, so she got fired. She labeled herself as a loser. She told her dad about it. The only response to her was a laugh and the line, "No, you're not. You'll figure it out. You've got what it takes, kid." This made her think if her dad was sure about it. Not one month after that, she got kicked out from the hockey team, she failed to be a part of the student government council, she even became a thief. Not to mention that she also used to get drunk.

Another conversation happened between her and her dad. She would blurt out all her failures and regrets. With all those horrible things that happened to her, Greenie only said, "This is all part of growing up. You're all right, Lovey", and "You're good enough. Trust me."

She held into those *You're good enough* words of her dad. Unfortunately, negative things still happened on her twenties and thirties. Her dad, who was intentionally blind of the things and blunders she had done, still would say, "I'm telling you, Lovey, you're gonna get there."

I Love You

Kelly says that when you love, you are ready to embrace the flaws of the ones you love. You love not because of the happy times and the good qualities of the persons you love. You do it because of all the awful things that happened between you and your parents, siblings, children, friends, and yourself that you have surpassed. You do it not because of the good things you're getting but the not so good ones you're experiencing and able to still love and be strong to forgive and forget and just enjoy the feeling.

According to her, when two people who have the same feeling use these words for the first time, it's electrifying. It's like a knock-me-off-my-feet moment. When these are used for a thousand times, it's a cause for marvel. It's creates an extremely good feeling, but when you hear it for the last time, it's like a dream or a music that you want to visit or listen to over and over again.

No Words At All

Cheers, dance moves, high fives, and emoji – these were some of the ways Kelly mentioned that replaced words to be spoken. They were used to communicate even without the help of any form of verbal communication. For her, the problem with language is that when you want to say something, you still need to arrange words into sentences through thinking, which requires focus. When looking for the exact words to say, sometimes it would take time until your feeling didn't match anymore with what you would want to say.

When Liz, Kelly's best friend, passed away, Kelly became silent and chose not to talk to people yet. She would just choose to sit and to spend the day with herself. She owed a lot of phone calls from concerned friends who would curiously ask how she was. Kelly just accommodated a few phone calls because, for her, the choice of words was a big deal. Words like *well*, *those poor kids*, and even *fuck cancer* had been questionable for her to hear.

It was summer before Liz passed away when their families had an exciting family adventure. Kelly witnessed the way Liz took care of her children. When everybody was busy, Kelly and Liz had a chance to talk. Liz shared her dream with her best friend. It was a dream of what happened when mothers died. She said that how all the mothers died would be on a colossal airplane where there were seats and rows set up on a glass floor where they could have the chance to see how their children would live out the future. She had the chance to see the mistakes and the flaws her children were making but the rule on that place was that you could only watch as much as you wanted but could only intervene once. Mistakes were made, which made her decide to intervene, but one of the mothers on that plane told her, "Not now. He'll figure it out. She'll come around." Liz, achingly told Kelly that her children didn't need her interventions, which meant they didn't need her on that dream.

Part of Kelly's routine was to volunteer at NICU to carry babies – babies who were sick, who were abandoned, and who were angelic. In the beginning, she worried about offending other mothers albeit it seemed inviting to carry a single baby. She met Bette, a staff in that hospital. She taught Kelly about the close silence – no lullabies and no baby talks, just close silence. Kelly felt the warmth and connection between her and the babies she carried. Many a time she would carry an angel, Bette would just remind her and whisper to her, "Close silence – that's all they need."

Kelly remembered what her daughter Georgia would request when she fetched her from school. No matter how excited and happy she was to see her mom, she would enjoy much more looking at the window while on their way home than telling her everything that she did in school because, for her, she was tired of the long hours of talking and answering people's questions.

With this, she realized to continue using the close silence in her life. It amazed her the possibilities of caring for and cheering for a child without even saying a word.

Onward

"Thank you for the food before us, the people around us, and the love between us." This was one of Liz's lines, which was used again and again by Kelly and the family who loved her dearly. When Liz passed away, Kelly thought that it was she who should make the connection between her family and Liz's. Little did she know, it was still her best friend's influence and memories that tied them all together.

Kelly wrote a sweet letter for Liz. It was actually like a journal where the momentous events were mentioned. With the annual tradition, the members of Kelly's and Liz's family would pass gifts to each other with the feeling of gratefulness, connectedness, and certainty that Liz was just around the corner.

Kelly had a short talk with Gwen, one of Liz's children. She asked her if it was hard hearing kids talking about their moms and their favorite things to do. Gwen nodded and together they cried for missing and longing for a mother and a friend very much. With Dru, Gwen, and Margo, Kelly informed Liz about each of them, each of their endeavors and successful moments. She would love and care for the kids as long as they let her and as long as she knew that Liz wanted these for Kelly to do.

Andy, Liz's husband, remembered and shared the conflicts and the ups and downs of their relationship, which made their marriage strong enough and intact. He spent numerous times thinking about how to celebrate or face the day of December twelfth, the first-year death anniversary. This was when the idea of annual tradition really commenced. He asked the closest friends of Liz's to write some memorable paragraphs, like a trivia, based on her pictures. Kelly chose the one revealing Liz as an exceptional athlete. Yearly, the tradition would continue until the kids knew their mother more and more and to prevent from forgetting her.

Kelly reminisced the time when she and Liz thought of what might happen when Liz died. They thought of the not so good things that might happen to him, including being drunk and mad with the children. What happened was totally different. He started reading. He attended grief counseling. He had swimming three times a week. He learned about cooking. He had walks with a friend where raising the children was the main topic.

Edward shared that Andy said, "No dad knows his kids like a mom does." Edward replied that he had a great relationship with Georgia and Claire. Andy clarified his stand by saying, "I know you do. I'm just saying you can't possibly know them as well as Kelly can." This involved a mothers' attitude of worrying too much and overthinking things.

Andy also thought about the possibility of having someone to sleep and wake up with. Then, one day, in Liz's spot of the bed, Gwen was there, reading. It made Andy think deeply. When he was about to sleep, he took his wife's bedside and decided that if there would be someone to sleep with him, they would take his old side.

Andy had a feeling of having a crush by which he thought it was quite like teenagers' stuff yet he assured that he was not ready yet. Kelly thought if it was possible that Andy would find the other one, this woman would definitely marry both Liz and Andy. Liz was within him always. She even wrote and left a letter for the future woman in her husband's life. He tried to take off his ring but hated what he did so he decided to put it back. He tried to be cautious of the people who would look for his wife and chose to just say, "I'm a single parent." To Kelly, however, he would explain that he was still married and this relationship would be and forever existed. He cried a lot remembering Liz, as if saying her name and telling things about her was like a mantra. He would

27

remember her in things that she did just like choosing to bake with his wonderful kids.

On the day Liz passed away, Andy was regretful not to witness it because he had to bring Gwen to her soccer game. Kelly, who was still there to comfort him, assured him that his wife died knowing that she was loved.

Kelly commended Andy with the way he handled things. She admired him by the two roles he had been doing – as a father and a mother when Liz left. She described him as an excellent student who would read and reread his wife's journals in order to learn and become the best parent he could be.

During the memorial, everyone lent their ears to Andy – wanting to listen to the amazing things he would say about Liz, to their love story, her motherly ways in taking care of their children, and the ways to move onward from loss. It was, for Kelly, the best thing she's ever heard about grief.

Almost on the last part of her letter, Kelly told Liz about the Apollo 13's mission where metaphor was widely used. It was about the astronauts who wanted to explore a portion of the Moon, but before the spacecraft reached it, there was an explosion and they needed to get back to Earth only with the help of the gravitational power of the Moon. Kelly compared Liz's loved ones to the astronauts who were in the ship trying to reach Liz as the Moon. With her death, that explosion happened, but it was through her that they learned also how to move onward with her own gravitational *power of love*. Kelly also said that Liz was JFK. She was the one who was in control of the program. She was the one who trained the people around her to pay attention, listen, think of themselves, set high standards, appreciate, savor the moments, and love.

At the end of the tear-shedding letter, Kelly assured Liz that her family was moving onward not from her but *with* her, just like what she did with her dad Greenie.

This Is It

Kelly's days when she got out of college were focused on the goal of adventure. She saved money to travel to different countries most people wished to go to. Time came when her money was enough that she needed not to work to have more.

Her travel goals were changed to a more serious matter when she headed into her thirties. She would dream of having healthy kids and a sensible man to be with. She dreamt of having an ideal family. However, it took a long time before she met the real love of her life.

When she finally had a family of her own (her husband Edward and daughters Georgia and Claire) and had the role called motherhood for a *very* long time, she wanted to go back to her old life, whether it was enjoying her teenage life or about to start being a mother of two cute little kids – no worrying about their whereabouts.

Albeit she had this attitude of I-want-to-go-back dream of hers, she also confessed that she liked the present time of her life despite the ups and more downs (the problems, the loss, the frustrations, the miscommunications, and the fights) in it.

There were times when she felt claustrophobic, limited of the freedom or being trapped with a room full of things to do. However, she learned to say *this is it* or *this is what my chosen life offers*. On and on, with an open mind and heart, she still chose to live and savor the moments that she had.

Conclusion

In life, it is indeed important to embrace and accept changes. *It's like this* pertains to showing the reality of what life has in store. Change, be it positive or negative, will always be a part of life. Instead of ranting about life issues, the word *accept* exists because it has to be used or has to be done.

To be interesting, you have to be interested. Listening is one effective way of letting people know that you care. When you listen, it doesn't necessarily mean that the person sharing needs your expertise or advice. Sometimes, he or she just needs someone to listen to him or her.

In life, no matter how grand you have planned, your future will still leave a question mark. *I don't know*, three words that need to be expressed and used in multiple possibilities, especially when you're not sure about life. It's true, your future will be a mystery. What will happen to you tomorrow? I don't know.

I hope you're okay, I'm sorry, Good luck, these are just some of the expressions we say to people who are encountering trials in their lives. Wouldn't it be more helpful if you would just say *I know*? Empathy. Empathy is needed in here. When you've learned to put yourself in the shoes of others, specifically the ones who needed it more, that's the only chance that they will appreciate and see that you understand where they're coming from.

Why is *no*, for a lot of people, a word that connotes a negative thought? Why are we afraid of saying what's on our minds? Sometimes, when we stop ourselves from saying something that we want, we just keep ourselves quiet and choose to say yes so there will be no further discussion about anything. Have the bravery to say *no*, not because you want to contradict or oppose but because you want this word to reflect your prudence, honesty, and dignity as a person.

Short but informative, Kelly had mentioned all of the things she did say *yes* to. What pleases us, what makes us happy, what challenges us in a positive way, whatever it is that gives us satisfaction and pleasure, we say *yes* to. Kelly, despite the things she was going through, she still had reasons to face life and shout out the things that make her happy.

From a book I once read, one of the lines said, *While we're busy growing up, we forget that they are growing old.* Kelly forgot about this; that's why her dad's lines reminded her. She had buried this guilt in her heart for not doing the things she could have done. As days passed, she realized that being wrong was not the same with being bad. Yes, she did not pay a visit but that's not actually the issue. What her father wanted her to realize was that in order to show love to people, you should also show this to the ones they love. Knowing deeply that person, getting to know more Cleta, her grandmother, was one way of showing Kelly's love to her and more to her dad.

Being wrong was not being bad at all. We just sometimes tend to be afraid of the line *I told you so*. How brave are those who admit that they're wrong and do the act of humility by saying *I was wrong*.

At the time she was forty years of age, Kelly became closer to her dad. She asked him about why every time she failed, he would still say that it was part of growing up. Her dad well explained to her that she didn't need to get everything right.

All the plans and things we want to achieve are sometimes not the ones that happen to us. We may fall down, we may fail, we may get fired because those are the things that might be meant to be felt in our journey. Despite the times that we face obstacles, there are still people who believe in our capabilities. Greenie believed in Kelly. Laura assured Ariel that she could do it. Rabbi Noa had faith in Ruby. Kelly's mother telling her that she was nothing if not competent.

The people who love us will listen to us all the time. They will tell us over and over again the things that they want to convey so that little by little we will understand their purpose. Being good enough doesn't mean that you are limited of the things that you can do. It's an eye opener that despite the failures, someone will assure you that there is something within you like a power that will let you discover and unfold your heart's desire.

When a person tells you that he or she loves you, I bet you definitely feel like in the seventh heaven. In the Spiderman show and in a lot of talks, it is indeed true that with great power comes great responsibility. Once you say that you love a person, you have the responsibility to show it or even prove it. This is the common view of the words I Love You.

What's new? It's forgiveness. No one is perfect - such a cliché but it's true. When your child does something wrong, will she or he not be your child anymore? When a student doesn't make it to the test, will the teacher just drop him or her out of school? No. What does love do with these situations? A parent forgives and corrects her child to do better. A teacher teaches again to help his or her student pass. Do you see the power of love? It automatically comes out when you learn to forgive.

Communication has two kinds. The first kind is the verbal

communication. This includes speaking, talking, or preaching in order to deliver a message. The second one is the non-verbal communication. This includes the body gestures, eye contact, or anything that is used to convey a message without speaking.

In this chapter, the saying *Action speaks louder than words* was emphasized. From the day Kelly grieved the loss of her friend, she mesmerized the days when she would see the *actions with love* her best friend would carefully do for her children. She also remembered the value of using the *close silence* in the hospital when taking care of the babies. She even reminisced the time when her daughter requested silence but with assurance that she was happy to see her mom.

People often say the line *less talk, less mistakes*. Does that mean no talk, no mistakes? No. The absence of words does not guarantee that people have no room for mistakes anymore. This chapter wants to open the eyes of the readers to know the time when to be a verbally or non-verbally person.

There are many ways by which non-verbal communication can be effective. When there is conflict, some people choose to be quiet and wait for the right time to approach the persons they've argued with. In the classroom, at the very first day of school, a teacher instructs the students with some routines and procedures in order to do things swiftly, like how to greet people, what is the signal when someone wants to go to the lavatory, the signal when the teacher wants the students to focus and be quiet, or even how to properly speak when confused with something that the teacher has said. A guidance counselor lets a shy student write or draw about their feelings toward the things that bother him or her. Even war stops and needs silence during *cease fire*.

Close silence, despite the loud world that people have, is indeed needed. It might convey a lot of messages so it needs a follow up when the person starts to speak up. Nevertheless, when time comes that explanations are not needed, people can freely show what they feel without using any spoken words for real.

What is the difference between moving on and moving onward? For others, when they say that they want to move on, they tend to do things they didn't do before, like trying something new or simply doing things to divert their attention. They move on *from* the persons or awful things that they have encountered or that have happened. They try to forget. That's why scenes like throwing or returning things happen or used to happen. When people move onward, on the other hand, they see the past as their guiding light. They move *with* the persons involved. Whether the reason is from the best or worst, people who move onward choose to remember what happened and treat their experiences as a guide for the better future.

Andy would never be the best husband he could be if he just chose to move on. Instead, his memories with his wife Liz made him move onward with her and his lovely kids. He chose the path for the better way to ease the pain of loss. He held into his faith and love to continue life and seize each day with the guidance of his beloved wife.

When we make hard decisions from very difficult situations, we use to say *this is it*. When a man finds the woman whom he fell in love with for a very long time and decides to make a proposal, though nervous and not sure of the answer, he will say *this is it*. When a patient who needs to undergo an operation, they would say a prayer and prepare himself or herself, they would also say *this is it*. In each moment, before a result comes out, *this is it* can come up with a variety of interpretations like *It's final*, *Good luck*, *God bless*, and more. It's like a signal of facing the climax of a story – a life story. With Kelly's life, though she kept on remembering the days of pleasures and aspirations, her own *this is it* meant that she's ready to face anything out of love for her dearest family.

Final Thoughts

Split. This is a movie that starred one of my favorite actors, James McAvoy. This is about a person who has multiple personalities. Each chapter in Kelly Corrigan's *Tell Me More* gives a wow impact to me or to whoever read, reads, and will read it. Each chapter made me split my personalities. Each personality made me learn new things to live by. I've become a mother, a wife, a daughter, a psychotherapist, a best friend, a cancer patient, a husband, and a parent.

It's like this. I am a mother who knows everyone in the family. I've become familiar with the role of each family member. I accept every member's differences. I accept each other's flaws even if it's impossible to take in.

Tell me more. I am a good listener who is willing to ask more questions, not to fish out some answers, but to let someone be open and expressive of what's on his or her mind. I am ready to listen and avoid myself to intervene with what my friend is telling me. I am just like a student who asks for more instructions and who thirsts for more learning without complaining.

I don't know. I am a cancer patient but a hopeful person that despite the challenges I face, I still turn down the word despair and choose possibilities out of impossibilities. I am brave to accept everything that is happening and willing to try and face life even if my tomorrow is still a mystery.

I know. I am a best friend who is always there for my friend in need either in laughter or even in the darkest of times. I am a friend who can relate with what my friend feels. I value empathy. I show compassion.

No. I am a daughter who knows when to follow and be satisfied when someone tells me to stop. I am a daughter who understands that mothers indeed know best. I am a person who is ready to accept rejections. I am also an individual who can boldly say *no* when in need to say *no*.

Yes. I am a jolly person with a lot of things I am grateful for. I am a cheerful person who says yes to things I enjoy the most. I am a happy person who treats things as blessings and not burdens.

I was wrong. I am an imperfect person who admits that no matter how careful I plan things ahead, I still have the capabilities of making mistakes and blunders. I am an imperfect person who courageously accepts the consequences of what I've done and tries to see in the future how better of a person I've become.

Good enough. I am a psychotherapist who is willing to listen to people's stories and concerns. I am trustworthy to be entrusted with things that are hard to tell. I am a person who accepts what I can and cannot do. I am a person who treasures people who do not stop believing in me. I learned to get motivated with the positive things that are happening.

I love you. I am a sincere individual who expresses my love to people not only because of the good things we have shared but also for the not so good moments or struggles that we have tried to surpass together. I am a sincere individual who always proves my love for those whom I love.

No words at all. I am a caregiver who commits to silence and peace and who is willing to lend a hand for the people who need me and my service, even without the use of any form of verbal communication, but more of actions, which speak louder than words.

Onward. I am a husband who is willing to accept loss and take courage to become a two-role parent without taking anything for granted. I am that husband who painstakingly does my responsibilities but dedicates my life to the people I love. I am a husband who remembers my beloved wife and all the things we've shared when she was still alive.

This is it. I am that self-actualized individual who seems satisfied with what happened, is happening, and will happen in my life. I am a mother who is ready to transcend everything for the betterment of the people I love.

This book has become my best buddy, which daily reminds me of the things that I should cherish and the words that I should use properly. This has been my constant reminder and my wake-up call when I'm in need of comfort. I've found a friend in this book, a friend that gave me pieces of advice through powerful words.

Speaking of words, words, words. One particular seminar I've attended talked about and focused on the most powerful thing in the world. The speaker asked everybody about their guesses on what that specific thing could be. Some said technology because it keeps on changing, upgrading, and updating. Others said the answer is prayer for the reason that it gives a person the chance to talk to God. No one got the right answer. When the speaker said it was actually words per se, everybody waited for an explanation.

Words are powerful because they have the capacity to make or break. Words can make when a person chooses the right things to say, or should I say, the positive things that people want to hear. Words can break when a person chooses the not so good ones to say or if he or she tells something that is very unpleasant to hear.

With Kelly Corrigan's *Twelve Hardest Things* she's learning to say, some of them seem making and some seem breaking. What makes them powerful? The stories behind those words make them powerful. What is my point here? Even a simple *I love you* can either make or break. These three words are very meaningful but they depend on the situation where they are used. Take this example. A man tells his girlfriend that he loves her. Unfortunately, the best friend of his girlfriend likes him, and when she hears these words told to another girl, she gets hurt and hopeless. I agree with Kelly that words that will turn into sentences should be carefully constructed because however good your intentions are, misunderstanding may come out.

Reading this book made me think of the quotes from the books I've read. I started to relate these quotes with Kelly's stories, words, and experiences. Here are some of them.

1. Pain demands to be felt. When Greenie passed away, Kelly couldn't help but hate Cancer the Enemy. She couldn't help but grief because of loss. This deep sadness of hers became deeper than before when, later, her best friend, Liz, passed away, too. (John Green, *The Fault in Our Stars*)

2. The world is not a wish-granting factory. Not *all* that Kelly planned in her life happened. Her life was full of ups and

downs, which made her understand and learn to be content of what she had. (John Green, *The Fault in Our Stars*)

3. When you know how to die, you know how to live. When Liz found out that she was dying of cancer, her, Kelly, and her loved ones cherished all the remaining days of hers by remembering the things that were worth remembering, and by savoring the moments that they had. (Mitch Albom, *Tuesdays with Morrie*)

4. Death ends a life, not a relationship. When Greenie and Liz passed away, Kelly still made ways to connect with them. She grieved because of loss but never forgot to make them alive in her by living with the things she had learned and acquired from them. (Mitch Albom, *Tuesdays with Morrie*)

5. The secret of life, though, is to fall seven times and get up eight times. On her early years of teenage life, Kelly faced a lot of rejections, failures, and frustrations. Albeit she got all of these, she still managed to succeed by letting her experiences as her guiding light and as lessons to live by. She learned to be positive out of all the negativities in life. (Paolo Coelho, *The Alchemist*)

6. When you want something, the entire universe conspires in helping you to achieve it. Kelly might have faced a lot of struggles or obstacles in life but miracles happened that she

was able to achieve what her heart desired. She had people around her who helped her to move onward and to be successful. (Paolo Coelho, *The Alchemist*)

7. The most beautiful things in the world cannot be seen or touched, they are felt within the heart. Love. Love with the people around her became the main reason where Kelly held into in order to live. (Antoine de Saint-Exupéry, *The Little Prince*)

8. Happiness is a journey, not a destination. Through her story, though faced with forlorn moments, Kelly did not just grieve but found reasons to be happy. She did wish for happiness and even looked for it, but unconsciously, it definitely came along her way. (Robin Sharma, *The Monk Who Sold his Ferrari*)

9. Investing in yourself is the best investment you will ever make. It will not only improve your life, it will improve the lives of all those around you. When willingness of hers to become a better person herself became evident, it did not only make her improve. It also affected her loved ones in positive ways. (Robin Sharma, *The Monk Who Sold his Ferrari*)

10. The moment I stopped spending so much time chasing the big pleasures of life, I began to enjoy the little ones. When faced with challenges, Kelly wished to go back to her

45

old life but she learned to face the truth. Turning down the things she wished to have and choosing the path of motherhood taught her how to be content of what she had. (Robin Sharma, *The Monk Who Sold his Ferrari*)

Indeed, I've learned a lot of things. Surely, I will treasure all of them and let them be my inspiration to fulfill my aspirations. I'll end my thoughts with Don Miguel Ruiz's first agreement: be impeccable with your words. Whatever your intentions are, speak with integrity; say what you mean; and use words with the guidance of truth and love.

About the Author

Throughout this book, I've known Ms. Kelly Corrigan more and more but from a blog that I've read, she is the director of The Nantucket Project. As I browsed the Internet about this project, I found out that its focus was the inspirational talks, short films, and unforgettable experiences about what matters most.

Kelly is a wife and a mother who continuously worries about her husband and her kids but constantly feels grateful about what is happening in her life.

She loves live performances such as good music, inspirational talks, and wonderful plays.

She still volunteers in a children's hospital and even creates a fundraising project to help out people who are in need.

She lives happily with Edward, Georgia, and Claire.

On top of this, she still misses her most beloved dad, Greenie.

Final Thoughts

Hey! Did you enjoy this book? We sincerely hope you thoroughly enjoyed this short read and have gotten immensely valuable insights that will help you in any areas of your life.

Would it be too greedy if we ask for a review from you?

It takes 1 minute to leave 1 review to possibly influence 1 more person's decision to read just 1 book which may change their 1 life. Your 1 minute matters and we value it and thank you so much for giving us your 1 minute. If it sucks, just say it sucks. Period.

FREE BONUS

P.S. Is it okay if we overdeliver?

Here at Abbey Beathan Publishing, we believe in overdelivering way beyond our reader's expectations. Is it okay if we overdeliver?

Here's the deal, we're going to give you an extremely valuable cheatsheet of "Accelerated Learning". We've partnered up with Ikigai Publishing to present to you the exclusive bonus of "Accelerated Learning Cheatsheet"

What's the catch? We need to trust you... You see, we want to overdeliver and in order for us to do that, we've to trust our reader to keep this bonus a secret to themselves. Why? Because we don't want people to be getting our exclusive accelerated learning cheatsheet without even buying our books itself. Unethical, right?

Ok. Are you ready?

Simply Visit this link: http://bit.ly/acceleratedcheatsheet

We hope you'll enjoy our free bonuses as much as we've enjoyed preparing it for you!

Free Bonus #2: Free Book Preview of Summary: Jab, Jab, Jab, Right Hook

The Book at a Glance

Gary Vaynerchuk likens doing business to boxing. The way a boxing match goes is closely similar to how businesses and consumers interact with each other. In the modern setting, of which social media marketing is an essential part, businesses jab their consumers by providing content that can entertain and inform. Depending on how the consumers respond, the business can then proceed to jab some more or go for a right hook, which is equated to the sale or closing of the deal. This engagement is what Gary believes to be the driving force between business-consumer interaction online and offline.

In this book, Gary intends to educate businesses and marketers, especially those with small businesses, in the way of social media marketing. With his expertise and experience from his own success and his clients' from VaynerMedia, he hopes to teach the reader how to succeed in getting their brand known by their target audience. In doing so, the reader will hopefully be able to capitalize and create results from effective offers and promotions done on social media platforms.

The first few chapters of this book delve on the current set-up of the world regarding use of mobile devices and social media networks. The progress of this evolution in media has happened in the same way in previous forms, particularly in print, radio, and television. He also iterates how the modern story-telling process works in marketing and how it was shaped to its current form by social media. Then, he enumerates valuable pointers on how to create valuable content that will be effective jabs to make your audience relate with your brand.

In the next part, he builds upon the characteristics of good content to provide insight on current best practices and effective marketing strategies on the most used social media platforms. Facebook, Twitter, Pinterest, Instagram, and Tumblr are tackled individually. For each of these platforms, the right kind of content is explained and some tips are given on how to create effective content native to the platform. He also explores the opportunities from some of the emerging social media networks.

Transitioning from the different social media platforms, he explains the importance of effort to achieve success in any area of life. He says that it is true that small businesses have a great disadvantage when it comes to resources. This greatly affects their capability to match the marketing efforts of bigger businesses. However, the disadvantage of being a small organization is an advantage in of itself as it enables such businesses to respond at a faster rate to their audience's needs, interests, and preferences. He reiterates that, depending on the quality of effort exerted, advantages such as capital, budget, and human resource can be overcome.

In the last part, he states that the requirements for success in the modern day are a lot more different than those in the past. This is mostly due to the technological and socio-cultural changes brought on by various modern advancements. More changes will occur and things will get more difficult. Nevertheless, in the scheme of things, this shouldn't be the problem if your mindset is that of constant learning and development to achieve and maintain the leading position. Having this mindset will equip you to always fight for that position and, in the process, you will constantly grow as a professional.

Introduction: Weigh in

Business, like boxing, has an aggressive, competitive, and fast-paced feel to it. This is no different in the world of social media marketing. Companies create big campaigns or promotions to create results that will give them advantage over their competition. Like the right hooks in boxing, they know that these events deliver sales and the return of investment for their business.

In the current setting, marketers create campaigns one after the other but they still fail in creating the results they are after. This failure is borne out of the assumption that, with a well-executed right hook, one can lessen or forego creating relationships with their customers. It would have worked in the age of television and digital media; however, social media has changed the dynamics of business-customer interaction.

Frequent and numerous promotional offers just do not work as much anymore as today's business; like boxing, it does not consist only of right hooks. Yes, often, only the right hook is seen as the punch that won the match. However, without the boxer (the business) delivering jabs (customer engagement), the delivery of the "right hook" would surely miss. Either the recipient of such promotions would ignore it or it will have no audience at all as it did not provide the requisite jabs for customer engagement.

The inspiration for this book came from the realization that Gary's success for Wine Library TV was a result of authentic and genuine content suited for YouTube. The author emphasized in his previous book, *The Thank You Economy,* and in his various speaking engagements that social media marketing should be done with the long-term in mind. There should be genuine and solid customer engagement as this will create active and real relationships with one's customers. However, as Gary realized, sales and return on investment cannot be achieved by only using customer engagement. There should be well-executed "right hooks", or campaigns and sales as well, to create the revenue that will spell success for the business.

In his first book, *Crush It!,* Gary taught the readers how to create great content and how to utilize content for the different platforms available at that time. Nevertheless, the changes in existing platforms and development of new ones have brought about the need to change past approaches to deliver successful right hooks in the current setting. With this book, all the knowledge from the first two books will be updated and combined to illustrate how to apply it in the current social media and digital environment.

Regardless of the type of company or organization you're in, your task is to tell the story of your organization, company, or brand to your customer. Especially now that what was done in print, radio, and television has a smaller audience as to what it used to before, and direct e-mails and banner ads are not as effective as before. The only option for the most effective marketing is through social media as this is where people spend most of their time now.

This book will set you up in how to tell your story on the most important social media platforms of the time. The storytelling formula will be taught to you so that your story will be effective delivering your message to your customers. An examination of some of the good, bad, and ugly stories done by different companies will be done to illustrate the common pitfalls in social media marketing. Once you've learn all this book can teach, you will be able to adapt to any new platforms in the future.

Jab, Jab, Jab, Right Hook is considered to be the last book in Gary Vaynerchuk's trilogy on the evolution of social media and of his career as a marketer and businessman. Although the world and the available platforms change, the secret to creating results remains the same. To attain brand awareness and profit through social media marketing, it requires the classic and everlasting values of hard work, passion, constant engagement, sincerity, long-term commitment, and clever and strategic storytelling.

Read More…

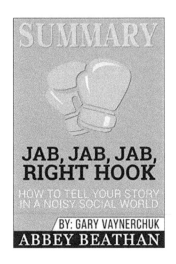

CPSIA information can be obtained
at www.ICGtesting.com
Printed in the USA
BVHW031548190619
551436BV00001B/106/P